Oubliette

A play

David Foxton

Samuel French — London
www.samuelfrench-london.co.uk

ISBN 978 0 573 12188 3

CHARACTERS

Anne Marston
Guide 1
Visitor 1
Visitor 2
Cath
Alison
Meg Warren
Jane
Liz
Rebecca
Mary Morton
Simon
Guide 2
Visitor 3
Susan Makem
James Darlow
Richard Darlow
Guide 3
Pastor Arnold
Guide 4
Dr Allenby
Mason

NB. The "Guide" roles can be played by two performers, by combining Guides 1 and 3, and 2 and 4.

Time—present day and the end of the 15th century.

OUBLIETTE

*An empty space: a room with a stony floor with some large stones or
small rocks. A cup of water is set at the rear of the stage. Two benches
are also at the rear and a smaller one* DL

The CURTAIN *opens on Anne wearing a grey puritan servant's outfit. She
moves slowly to* C *and looks up. She puts her arms out to the sides and
turns round slowly twice, then with her arms by her sides she rolls her
head, hunches and works her shoulders, then stands motionless and
screams loudly, piercingly. She freezes as she listens, then she moves to
the rear of the "room" and paces forward, measuring the space, then
to her right, measuring again with paces. Her mouth moves as she
counts but we hear nothing. She repeats the measuring process, this
time using her feet as the measure — again we see her mouth move
but nothing is heard*

*A Guide, dressed in period costume, enters with a small group of
present-day visitors*

Guide Just mind your heads as you come in ... this is the oldest part of
the building. Our historians date it as early as the twelfth century ...

When Anne speaks neither the Guide nor the visitors look at her

Anne There's always been a manor house here ...
Guide You'll notice that it is a completely windowless room ...
Anne ... no need for windows ...
Guide ... indeed until the Trust took the whole site over six years ago
there was no door into this room either ...
Anne ... no need for a door ...

Guide It may seem incredible but in fact until the Trust surveyed the property this room was unknown. A truly secret room ... The entrance that we've just used was created shortly after the survey was done ...

Anne A forgotten room.

Visitor 1 So what was its use?

Guide Well it could have been a hiding place — we're used to buildings of this age having "priest-holes" — and of course during the Civil War many supporters of the King had to hide from Cromwell's troops ...

Visitor 2 If there was no door how did anyone get in?

Guide If you look up at the North Wall you can just see the vague outline of a small opening. This was seemingly closed up many years ago ...

Anne It was cold ... damp ... dark ...

Guide ... and this room ... was left. Prior to that it could have been an armoury or even a valuables store ... or a prison ...

Anne ... a prison ...

Guide We are still researching the possibilities, but it does seem possible that this room was an "oubliette": prisoners were put, or perhaps thrown, into this room through that small opening up there ... and then ... just left ...

Anne ... left ... just left ...

Visitor 2 To die ... you mean ... left to die?

Guide They were forgotten — hence the term "oubliette" from the French "oublier": to forget.

Anne ... never to recall ... never to be remembered.

Visitor 2 But surely there would be some evidence of prisoners having died in here. When the room was discovered ... weren't there any ... well ... bones ... or —— ?

Guide Our researchers did discover two shallow graves in the far corner of the room ... and two skeletons ... you can see them in the museum next to the shop on your way out ...

Anne Susan Makem and James Darlow.

Guide As yet they've not been identified, but were probably some enemies of the lord of the time. Now if we can just go back to the lower hall we need to continue the tour ...

Visitor 1 So who buried them?

Guide What?

Visitor 1 Who bothers to bury the people you have thrown in here to forget ...?

Guide There's still a lot of research work being done .... can we move on please ...?

The Guide and visitors begin to move out

Anne ... someone who cares ...

Guide ... and watch the step too ...

   The Guide and visitors exit

Anne ... someone who doesn't forget ...

There is a noise, off: someone bangs their head and shouts "Ow"

Guide (*off*) ... and your head ... please take care ...

Anne ... someone who was there.

The Lights change

   Alison enters and sits. Cath creeps on behind her. They are dressed similarly to Anne

Cath Boo.

Alison Don't do that.

Cath Made you jump, eh?

Alison Have you seen Mary?

Cath She'll be on her way ...

Alison They'll miss me if I'm not back soon.

Cath Same with me ...

   Meg enters, with Jane, Liz and Rebecca. They too are dressed as servants

Meg One of these days I'll kill that Pastor Arnold ... I will, I swear it ...

Alison What's he done now?

Meg Leering and gawpin' all the time ... he spies on me ... dirty old man ...

Jane You shouldn't say things like that.

Liz Sometimes I think I'll run away.

Rebecca Who with?

Liz No ... just away ... go to London, be a lady's maid there ... not just a skivvy round here ... pinchin' things to get my own back.

Alison What yer got then?

Jane Show us.

Liz Never you mind.

Rebecca I got a lace hanky ... real good quality — look.

Alison That cost a bit ... won't it be missed?

Rebecca Bottom of a trunk — forgotten about.

Mary Morton, another servant girl, enters

Mary Come on then — let's be having you — what have your sticky little fingers picked up for me today? One handkerchief then, Rebecca, is that it?

Rebecca It's a good one.

Alison I've got two, Mary — they'll be good for a penny, eh?

Jane I've got one as well, Mary.

Mary We'll see — I've got to do the selling — you provide, I sell, then we'll see. (*To Anne*) And where've you been hiding?

Anne Nowhere ... I've just been on my way ...

Rebecca You're a dreamer you are, Anne Marston, a real dreamer.

Anne We were busy up at the hall.

Rebecca More guests is it, from down south?

Jane They're from London, aren't they, Anne?

Anne That's it — family. And Master James needed some errands doing.

Mary Master James! When he calls, you jump. What've you brought?

Alison When he whistles you move quickly enough then.

Meg Reckon you've taken a fancy to your Master James Darlow.

Anne That's not so ... and I couldn't bring anything ...

Mary Did you try?

Anne I'll maybe get a chance when the guests go ...

Meg He's too high and mighty for you ... he's not our class ... there's no point in running around after him like a lapdog.

Mary You know the rules — you take — I pay.

Rebecca James Darlow's not lookin' to our kind.

Mary Find someone in the village ... that's what I've done ...

Liz One of your "buying" friends, is it?

Jane I'll bet it is — what's he called?

Anne Who? ... Who've you found then, Mary?

Mary I can't remember his name ...

Meg Good thing too 'cos she'll find another at the weekend.

Jane She usually does.

Mary What d'you mean by that?

Liz You're too generous, Mary — that's what she means.

Meg Sharing your favours around ...

Mary What d'you mean by favours? ... What are you suggestin'?

Meg I saw you with that Tom Sugden.

Liz And I saw you with Hugh Marlow's lad — Mark.

Jane Yes — I did as well — twice.

Mary Nothing wrong in being friendly.

Anne Nothing at all ...

Mary Always been friendly — our family — you ask anyone ...

Alison Her mother was *too* friendly, I've heard.

Mary Watch your tongue, Alison — don't speak out of turn.

Alison It's common knowledge.

Rebecca — aye — common's the right word, too ...

Mary Are you meaning me? ... Are you? ... Well? ... *Are you*?

Rebecca If the cap fits ...

An argument ensues

Simon, a young servant boy, enters

Simon Hey, you lot ... is Meg Warren here?

Alison Should she be?

Mary What's it to you?

Rebecca Snoopin' round ...

Simon Pastor Arnold's lookin' for her. She's in trouble.

Meg What sort of trouble?

Simon Don't ask me — ask Pastor Arnold, he knows and I don't ... but he's been checking on the choir's vestments ... I know that.

Meg He checked them — last week — he doesn't do it every week — he doesn't.

Mary You're not daft enough to pinch from the church are you, Meg?

Meg What d'you care? You take stuff wherever it comes from.

Mary I've never had no vestments — cut my throat and hope to die.

Meg I haven't passed it on yet ... I've got it squat.

Simon Pastor's after you, Meg ... you'd better get it put back ...

Meg I'll say I took it to mend.

Meg exits

Jane I'll bet he won't believe you.

Simon You're all gonna get caught out one day — they'll hang you, Mary Morton.

Mary If everyone keeps their traps shut, no one will ever get nabbed ... (*She grabs Simon*) ... and I mean everyone. (*Pause*) And if things do start turning badly I'll blame somebody else ... (*She looks around*) ... now who shall I blame?

Cath Susan Makem ...

Alison Yes, blame Susan — she knows no better ...

Rebecca She's yonderly ...

Simon I saw her just now — up on the crags — mucky as ever ...

Mary (*thinking*) ... Susan Makem.

Cath She's odd, she is ...

Jane You want to keep away from her.

Simon And she was singing ...

Anne She should be pitied.

Mary She should be locked up — she's as daft as a tree.

Anne She's no family ...

Rebecca She lives down at Parslow's farm — Mother Parslow feeds her scraps ...

Alison She lives with the pigs — I've seen ——

Simon — I've smelled ... certainly pigs all right ...

Guide 2 enters with a small group of present-day visitors. The Guide is in period costume

The onstage action freezes as they enter

Guide 2 Do be careful of the step ... and mind your head ... it's a recent doorway but it's rather low — this part of the manor is the oldest ... the Trust's historians believe it to be of twelfth-century origin. Little is known of its use — it was certainly well hidden within the fabric of the main building ... a secret room ...

Visitor 3 Isn't there some story about it? Isn't it haunted?

Guide 2 People always create stories of hauntings in buildings of this age ... I think it adds to the charm of history ...

Visitor 3 So no ghosts, then?

Guide 2 I'm afraid not, just an enclosed space ...

Anne What about the graves ...?

Guide 2 ... but we are continually researching. Who knows what might be discovered ... or uncovered.

Anne The bones were taken away ... taken away ...

Guide 2 We'll join the main tour again now ... there's really nothing more to see in here ... please take care as you go out ...

Guide 2 and the visitors move off and exit

Anne half-follows them

Anne Where's the story gone? What about it...?

Alison (*with a shriek*) Look! ... Look there!

Mary What is it? (*She bends to look*)

Liz Don't touch ... don't touch it.
Rebecca What is it?
Simon It's Susan Makem.
Mary It's a toad.
Simon Same thing.
Cath Kill it!
Jane Yes — kill it! Kill it!
Anne No! ... Leave it ...
Simon Looks like Susan Makem to me.
Rebecca Don't get too close. They spit, you know.
Simon So does Susan Makem ...
Cath I hate them ... kill it! ... Kill it now!

Mary picks up a rock and makes to kill the toad

Susan enters

Susan (*as she enters*) Don't be doing that, Mary Morton.
Simon Talk of the devil ...
Mary What?
Susan Put it down ... toads don't harm ... (*She bends to it*) Go home now ... these folks don't know you ... they're feared of you ... go home.

The girls react as the toad hops past them

Rebecca Toad spit can blind you ...
Susan You talk rubbish.
Cath They give you warts an' all ...
Alison One of them killed my auntie's baby ...
Susan You know nothin' ... you talk about things you know nothin' about ...
Mary And *you know* do you, Susan Makem?
Susan I know toads don't sting ... and I know you're a thief, Mary Morton.
Mary I never pinched nowt ——

Susan — you steal people, you get 'em to thieve for you. I knows what goes on ... I seen you all at it ... you'll end up on the gallows ... you'll be swingin' on the end of a rope ...

Mary Nobody'll believe you — you're a mad woman — the whole countryside knows it ...

Susan ... and the birds'll peck your eyes out.

Mary You don't know what you're talking about ——

Simon She knows about toads ...

Susan ... and I know a bad apple when I sees one.

Mary You mean me, Susan Makem? Is that me? Is it?

Susan One word from me in the right place and —— (*She turns away from Mary*)

Mary attacks Susan and knocks her to the ground, hitting at her — the rest are shocked, stunned. Perhaps only Simon tries to prevent the attack

Mary (*attacking*) You keep your mealy mouth shut, Makem — you say nothin' — nothin' ... (*She picks up the rock with which she would have hit the toad and hits Susan with it several times*)

Pause. Susan lies still

Simon Look what you've done, Mary ... (*He stoops over Susan*)

Rebecca Is she all right?

Mary That's shown her. That's a lesson she won't forget ...

Alison Is she dead? Is she? (*Pause*) What if she's dead?

Mary Shut it! ... Say nothing!

James Darlow and his brother Richard enter

James So here you are, Anne Marston. I've been calling you all over the —— (*He sees Susan*) What's happened here? (*Pause*) Well?

Mary She fell, Master Darlow. We were all here just talking, and this Susan Makem came up, all singing and far away ... and ... and ... this toad ... jumped out and scared her, and she fell, hit her head on this rock.

Pause

James Toad, you say? Is this true? (*Pause. He looks round*) Is this true,
   Anne? (*Pause*) Was there a toad?
Anne (*after a short pause*) Yes ... there was a toad ...

Richard looks to Susan

Richard She's badly hurt, James. Shall we call for the doctor?
James Dr Allenby's over at Skipton ... we'll take her back to the hall.
Richard But she's filthy, James ...
James We can't leave her here — she needs attention — If you won't
   carry her I will ... (*He lifts Susan*) ... who do you say she is?
Mary Susan Makem, sir ... and she's a troublemaker.
James Come on, Richard, and you too, Anne. There's no time to wait
   around — she's very pale.

James and Richard exit with Susan

Mary (*grabbing Anne*) Not a word — remember, not a word, or I
   shall finger you all.

Guide 3 enters in period dress

The action on stage freezes

Guide 3 (*to the audience as if they are visitors*) Careful, I know it's
   awkward, if you could just move over a little ... and if you're at
   the back perhaps you could just ease forward slightly. This part
   of the building is the oldest section, dating from the middle of the
   twelfth century ... it's a room enclosed by all the rooms around it
   ... a secure space ... discovered relatively recently ... it's not clear
   where exactly the original door was ...
Anne They took her back to the hall. Master James carried her back.
   His brother Richard said he was a fool, that he should have left her. I
   looked after her ... washed her, bathed the wound ... The doctor came
   ... she slept ... a deep sleep ... days of sleep ...

Guide 3 So we need now to retrace our steps — back to where we were.

Guide 3 goes

Mary Do you understand? She fell. She hit her head ... that's what happened. All right?

Mumbled assent all round

Simon It has nothing to do with me ....
Mary It has *now*!

Pastor Arnold enters dragging Meg

Arnold Who? Which one? You were going to give it to who?
Meg I was going to mend it, Pastor Arnold ... to mend it.
Arnold Don't you dare lie to me, Meg Warren. It was found in your room ... hidden away. You meant to sell it ... now tell me who was going to sell it for you ... is it one of you?
Mary (*innocently*) Has something happened, Pastor Arnold?
Arnold Who are you?
Mary Mary Morton if it please you.
Arnold I'm far from pleased, there's been thieving going on in the village — thieving from decent homes, even thieving from the church. And this Meg Warren is involved, I feel sure — but she isn't the only one. I mean to find out the truth.

Arnold and the girls exit. Anne remains

At the Hall, James and Richard enter to the bench DL

Richard She can't continue to stay here.
James And why not ... she's still not fully recovered — she was unconscious for over a week ...
Richard There's already talk in the neighbourhood.

James Gossips — let them talk ... she's a pretty thing, that's why ...

Richard Aye that's the reason all right — you've taken a liking to her
— that's why she's still here. It's nigh-on a month now ... the Fosters
were visiting when you brought her here — you recall, they came
up from London ...

James What sort of Samaritan are you?

Richard I'm not one at all. I just think she should be back with her
own people.

James And if she has none?

Richard Then ... well ... then ... out, just out. Anywhere. Let her fend
for herself like she obviously did before.

James She recalls nothing of the event — her mind is not fully sound
again.

Richard They say in the village that it never was.

Richard goes out

James remains, apart from the main area. He sits down DL

Cath enters to the main area, followed by Liz

Liz (*to Cath*) What're you doing here?

Cath I've got some stuff for Mary.

Liz You fool ... what are you playing at? You know the Pastor's on to
things ... and you're still pinching stuff.

Cath It was easy, my mistress never notices ... it's easy ... anyway
what're *you* waiting here for?

Liz Mary owes me money ...

Cath (*after a pause*) Do you think she'll come?

Liz She'd better ...

Rebecca enters

Rebecca (*as she enters*) No sign of Mary then? Is she coming?

Cath Have you got stuff for her?

Rebecca Mind your own ... have you?

Alison enters

Alison (*as she enters*) Listen, have you seen Meg? I just passed the pastor's house and you could hear screaming and shouting. I reckon Meg's getting a real beating.

Rebecca I heard it as well.

Liz She won't talk.

Abi I hope not — or we're in trouble.

Rebecca I'm scared — did you see the way the Pastor looked? He's got really piercing eyes ...

Cath You've nothin' to fear ... if we keep our mouths shut.

Alison I wish I'd never started ...

Rebecca Let's hope that Susan Makem says nothin'.

Mary enters

Mary (*as she enters*) Now then ... who's got what? (*Pause*) Well now ... who's first, eh?

The girls group together and hold their position

Anne comes forward to James

Anne Sir, I've brought Susan as you asked.

James Thank you, Anne ... bring her in.

Anne exits and then escorts Susan in. Susan is dressed smartly now, but is bewildered

You can leave us now, Anne.

Anne Sir?

James I'll call you if there's need ...

Anne retreats but remains on stage

Come, Susan. Sit here.

Susan I need to thank you ... sir.

James Thank me?

Susan The girl ... er ...

James Anne.

Susan Yes, Anne ... says I owe you my life ... you brought me here she says, after ... after ... I fell ...

James Do you not recall ...?

Susan I cannot remember it. She says I'm called ——

James Susan.

Susan Yes, Susan, but I can't think it ... my mind is foggy ... my memory ——

James — will come back ... give it time ... and rest...

Susan You are ... good ... to me ... sir.

James James.

Susan Yes ... you have looked to me.

James And I will... and now you must rest more — (*calling*) Anne!

Anne (*coming forward from the rear*) Sir?

James Take Susan back to her room. Let her sleep.

Anne Sir.

James Oh ... just one thing ... her dress ... did you find that for her?

Anne No, sir ... the London visitors sent it for her ... on their return they sent a parcel of clothes ...

James I see. Perhaps you should see if there's anything in the parcel you would like.

Anne has probably already helped herself

Anne Thank you, sir ... I will ... I will. Oh, and Pastor Arnold is waiting to see you ... shall I ask him to come up? He says it is urgent ...

James Everything is always urgent to Pastor Arnold — yes, Anne, send him up.

Anne Sir.

Anne escorts Susan off. She ushers in Pastor Arnold, who carries a bible

Anne remains onstage to the rear

The girls go off

Arnold Forgive the intrusion, Master James, sir, but it is an urgent and important matter.

James Well?

Arnold Sir, you may well not be aware of a spate of thieving that has beset our village, and indeed our neighbouring villages.

James I know nothing of such activities. What is missing — cattle? Sheep? Valuables?

Arnold Linen, sir.

James Linen? Stealing linen?

Arnold It would seem that maidservants have been encouraged to take linen from their households ... which has then been sold on.

James This is petty stuff, penceworth, surely?

Arnold Sir, theft is theft ... pence perhaps, but it all adds up ... and church items have been taken from the vestry.

James It's a matter for the constable ... how does it concern me?

Arnold Meg Warren who works for me is implicated, I believe — I have tried to wrest the truth from her but she is stubborn and admits to nothing ...

James So?

Arnold There's a group of girls involved — she hinted as much — one is your Anne Marston.

James Anne? I don't believe it of her.

Arnold Sir, if you were to speak to them all ... I think you might gain the truth. They respect you, sir ...

James And they don't respect *you*?

Arnold Sir ... I'm at my wits' end with this matter. It's a month or more since I began to ask questions of Meg and I'm no further forward.

James Very well ... I'll arrange to see them ...

Arnold They're here now, sir, I took the liberty of saying you wished to see them ... I have them with me.

James Quite a liberty, Pastor Arnold — but what is done is done — very well, I'll speak to them ...

Arnold Sir!

Pastor Arnold ushers the girls and Simon in

Meg has a black eye and considerable bruising to her face and mouth.
The girls and Simon stand in a group — uncertain, uncomfortable ...

James Which is Meg?

The girls push Meg forward

> This is a serious business, Meg, if what the Pastor tells me is true. Is
> it ...?

Meg looks about her ... but fails to speak

> Do you understand, Meg? Are you guilty of theft or not guilty?

Meg I'm saying nothing ... sir.

James A refusal to plead ... well now, Meg, if this were the constable's
court such a refusal would mean a punishment. Do you know that,
Meg? You would be pressed ... weights put on you until you did
plead. Now do you want me to call the constable to take you into
custody?

Meg (*after a pause*) It wasn't me.

James If you say it wasn't you ... then you imply it was someone else
... who? Who was it?

Meg looks at the others. There is a pause

> Who?

Anne (*entering the group*) ... All of us ... sir!

James What?

Anne We were all involved ...

The others deny it vociferously. Only Meg holds back. We hear Simon's
voice saying "not me" ... "it was the girls"...

James Quiet! Be quiet! Or it will be a court matter. So, Anne, you say
everyone was involved in this pilfering ... but who was the leader?
Who sold the goods you stole? Which one of you ...?

They all look at Mary ... and then wish they hadn't

> (*To Mary*) Was it you? Do I know you? ... Did you lead the others
> on? Persuade them to steal?

Susan wanders on and stands apart from the others

Mary No, sir! Not me, sir.

James Who, then?

Mary (*pointing at Susan*) It was her ... Susan Makem ... I swear it ...
she'd come to collect things when ... when she fell ... and you came
upon us, sir. Ask her ... go on, ask her ...

James She has yet to recover her memory of that day.

Mary She's lying ... it was her made us do it.

James *Made* you ... and just how did she *make* you?

Mary (*after a brief pause for thought*) Witchcraft, sir ... she said she'd
curse us ... she threatened us ... didn't she ...?

The others agree — it's a way out

Meg None of us would have done it but she witched us ...

Mary Just like she witched those pigs at Parslow's farm.

James She made them thieves too?

Mary No, sir ... she blighted them ... a whole litter died, sir ——

Liz (*warming to the lying*) — and she gave me these warts, sir ... look.
(*She bares her arm*)

Alison She poisoned Atkinson's sheep ...

Mary She's evil ...

James This looks like a job for you after all, Pastor — possession is
scarcely my concern ...

Anne It's not true, sir — Mary Morton's lying ... Susan was no part
of it ...

*Susan comes forward and points at Mary. It is dramatic — it could be
that she recalls Mary as her assailant — it is an accusation of such
perhaps. After a pause, Mary looks about and clutches her throat ...
then collapses slowly*

Arnold (*aghast*) Witchcraft!

Black-out. Screams can be heard

  Pastor Arnold, James and the girls, except Anne, go off

The Lights come up

  Allenby and Guide 4 in period costume enter to C

Guide 4 (*to the audience*) There has been considerable debate and
  research done by the Trust about this room, ladies and gentlemen
  — its intended use and indeed its actual use. Twelfth century origin
  certainly — but what else is known?

  Guide 4 moves out forward L

  Pastor Arnold enters to Allenby

Arnold (*very worried*) This business grows ... more girls fall ill ... this
  is undoubtedly the devil's work ... I have written fully to the Bishop.
  There must be an exorcism ... that Susan Makem creature is at the
  core, I feel it ... she must be tested, she must be thoroughly tried — this
  evil has to be rooted out. Don't you agree, Doctor?
Allenby I see no satanism, Pastor — but there is illness, that's a fact.
Arnold (*reading from his bible*) "Whoso causeth the righteous to go
  astray in an evil way, he shall fall himself into his own pit: but the
  upright shall have good things in possession." I can taste the sulphur
  — I feel the devil's breath.
Allenby You may see witches, Pastor — I see the sickness — the black
  swellings, the foul tumours, the open sores that follow and the fever
  that ravages and consumes ... and brings a pain-racked death.

  Richard and James enter L

Richard You must hand her over, James. The church will demand it —
  she has to be examined ...

James She is ill. Her memory is still lacking — she cannot think clearly, — she cannot reason ... how could she stand examination?

Allenby She's far from good, Master James — she is weak from the fall ... I have bled her as much as I dare. I cannot put the leeches to her again. I can only suggest rest and care — there is much illness about.

Richard They believe her possessed ——

James — and I do not.

Richard You are over-protective. They will come for her and you will be obliged to hand her over. You cannot deny the church ... if you dare refuse then perhaps the finger of witchcraft will point at you ... at us. You cannot risk that. We can be ruined by such accusations. I don't want to see that happen — not for some raggle-taggle girl who has charmed you — is that it? Has she charmed you? Is that part of her sorcery?

James The girl stays. While I am master here what I say stands — I'm not to be threatened — by them or by you.

James exits

Anne comes forward. Richard grabs her

Richard Tell me — how is the mad girl?

Anne Sir?

Richard The girl! The girl! Don't pretend you don't know who I'm talking about — my brother's fancy ...

Anne Sir?

Richard pushes Anne away roughly

Richard Dr Allenby — what is happening here? Are we all witched?

Allenby There is suffering and there is fever — but whether it is caused by witchcraft I know not. Illness abounds and shows no response to my treatments ... I fear for the village. This pestilence will become worse before it clears — but I don't intend to stay to see it run its course. I leave tonight for London. I would advise you to keep clear of anyone with a fever if you want to survive ...

Allenby exits, followed by Arnold. As they go they adjust the rear benches to become a bed. Richard also exits

James enters

James Anne!

Anne comes to James

Anne, you know the state of things. Susan is accused — voices speak against her. Pastor Arnold has a fervent, fanatical look in his eye. He smells demons and I think will not be satisfied until he sees them. They will come for her, and she is too ill to answer. Her illness will not help her, and my brother is running scared.

Anne Others *do* fall ill, sir. It's not just Mary Morton ... sir.

James I need your help ... I shall take Susan into the inner space — I'll show you where it is ... there's a small way in, and the room is completely hidden. *You* will know where she is — and I will know — but no one else. We can take food and water there — the matter will blow over, or she will recover in time to answer her accusers. Will you do this for me?

Pause

Anne Of course, sir ...

James goes

... for you.

Guide 4 At some time it was occupied ... perhaps only briefly. Items found suggest food was held here — was it some kind of prison?

Susan enters with a blanket on to the "bed" at the rear of the stage

Anne goes to Susan

Anne Lie still. Try to rest more ... keep warm.

Susan Stifling ... it's so warm ... water ... I need a drink ...

Anne (*picking up the cup of water*) Here, drink ... but just sips ... just
  sip the water.

Susan My throat burns ... I must drink ... and there's pain ... my eyes
  ... such pain. (*She lies back*)

Guide 4 ... or ... it could have been used for isolation — in the case
  of illness ... especially the more infectious type — smallpox or ...
  plague. Local records tell of an isolated outbreak of the plague in
  the fourteen-hundreds — probably brought to the village via fleas in
  clothing sent from London. Several young girls died ... and the local
  minister, Robert Arnold. James Darlow, the master of the house, is
  recorded as missing at the same time — though no record of his actual
  death exists — his brother, Richard, took over the estate.

James enters

James (*to Anne*) How is she today ...?

Anne She has a fever, sir ... she needs fresh air ... we should take her
  out of this place ...

James I cannot risk it. Fever abounds. She's better here.

Anne Her condition is worse, sir. Her breathing's very shallow ... she
  cannot swallow ... her neck is swollen — see ... (*indicating*) ... here
  and here ... and there's a rash. She should see a doctor ...

James No. It's not safe — the cry of "witchcraft" is everywhere ... and
  since Pastor Arnold fell ill, the Bishop has seen fit to send two of his
  keenest deacons to seek out the truth among us ... we must wait...
  wait. (*He coughs*)

Anne Drink some water, sir.

James Thank you, Anne. I know I can depend on you. (*He coughs*)
  Perhaps I'll rest here tonight ... my bones ache ... we have food
  here?

Anne Enough, sir ... rest.

Guide 4 Brother Richard had control of the household and the land —
  he signed orders on James's behalf and had control of the monies. He
  spent considerable amounts on building work.

Richard enters with the Mason. They move forward L

Richard What's the delay? Why the hold up in the work above the Lower Hall?

Mason The men are worried for their families ... if it's not the witch hunt it's the sickness ... some are ill themselves.

Richard I want that inner wall finished today. Put all available men to it — the walls that are there need doubling, and any passages, or holes, or entries in the old wall are to be sealed — walled up tight. There's nothing in the old walls that need concern us.

Richard exits, followed by the Mason

Anne He knew. He knew we were there. He had us walled up. He took James's place.

James (*weakly*) Are you ... still here, Anne? ... Anne?

Anne I'm here, sir ... with you ...

James ... and Susan ... Anne, what of Susan?

Anne She's ... she's gone, sir. (*She covers Susan with the blanket*)

James It's dark ... so dark ... (*He coughs*)

Anne I'll take care of you, sir ... I'll be here ... sir.

Guide 4 (*taking a more central position*) That was when we believe this room was closed up. Richard's building work completely hid any access to this room. If you could all move through a little more ...

The cast enter as more modern-day visitors. These visitors mask Susan and James

Susan and James leave the stage, unseen

You may well be aware that two shallow graves were discovered in here ... the bones have been removed for further examination and dating ... but they could be from that period of the fourteen-hundreds. Who was responsible for burying them remains a mystery. The Trust is about to embark on some major construction work on the adjacent hall and it will entail this old section being sealed once again ... so in fact you are the last visitors who will stand in this room for some time. If you would please now return to the lower hall... please be careful of the step, and mind your heads ... come along now, we don't want to leave anyone in here ...

All exit except Anne

Anne stands C, *solitary*

Anne ... I'm here ... I'm still here ... I'll always be here, Master James ... for you ...

The Lights fade to Black-out

FURNITURE AND PROPERTY LIST

On stage: Large stone or small rock
Three benches
Cup of water

Off stage: Lace handkerchief (**Rebecca**)
Two lace handkerchiefs (**Alison**)
Lace handkerchief (**Jane**)
Bible (**Pastor Arnold**)
Blanket (**Susan**)

LIGHTING PLOT

Practical fittings required: nil
One interior. The same throughout

To open: General interior lighting

Cue 1	**Anne**: "... someone who was there." *The lights change*	(Page 3)
Cue 2	**Pastor Arnold**: "Witchcraft!" *Black-out*	(Page 18)
Cue 3	The girls except **Anne** exit *Bring up lights*	(Page 18)
Cue 4	**Anne**: "... Master James ... for you ..." *Fade to black-out*	(Page 23)

EFFECTS PLOT

Voices and sounds heard from off stage can be supplied by actors

No cues

Printed by The Kingfisher Press, London NW10 7AS